NAME: _____

DATE: _____

This one ♡ is for you

WERK 101

GET-YOUR-LIFE
TOGETHER

WRITTEN BY
KOEREYELLE GUIDE

HEALTH, WEALTH, & LIFESTYLE LESSONS
FOR MODERN-DAY WOMEN

Werk 101: Get-Your-Life-Together Guide

Copyright © 2015 by Koereyelle DuBose

ISBN 978-0-9837182-4-6

Library of Congress Cataloging-in-Publication: 2015951324

Perfectly Imperfect Publishing Company

Printed in the United States of America

THIS ONE IS FOR YOU

Ready to get your life together once and for all? Well, look no more, you've picked up the right handbook. This book is dedicated to the modern-day woman who is dedicated to herself. She is a woman who wants more in life, sees a brighter future, and dares to dream big. She is a woman who is ready to stop wishing that her dreams will come true and start WERKing to achieve her goals, and live a life full of healthiness, wealthiness, and happiness.

INTRODUCTION

" *Don't be the woman with the most to say and the least to offer.* **"**

- *Koe*

YOU ARE A GAME-CHANGER. You are the one the world has been waiting for, and this guide was created with YOU in mind. Even past mistakes and bad occurrences can't stop a modern-day woman who is ready to *WERK* toward a more fulfilling, happier life. Get ready to let go of your old mentality and be liberated as I show you how to create a powerful, positive mindset, prepare for the man you've been praying for, and design your life's destiny on your own terms.

This book isn't meant to be read in one sitting. Instead I encourage you to *WERK* through it at your own pace, giving yourself time to digest and apply the newly found information. You'll find random lifestyle lessons, quick reference lists, journal activities (labeled as Let's *WERK!*), and plenty resources to **get-your-life-together** and take you one step closer to becoming the woman you're meant to be, a Queen — the one God created you to be.

Whether you "think" a lesson applies to your life or not, be open-minded and complete it. Then watch how an opportunity to use your new knowledge will present itself like magic.

These important steps will help make this handbook *WERK* for you:

- As you come to an affirmation, I challenge you to speak it aloud and really let it resonate in your spirit.
- Take your time going through the *WERK*sheets, lessons, and exercises. It's better to complete them thoroughly with a clear mind than to rush through them. Let them *WERK* for you! Be real with yourself

so that you truly can develop into the best version of yourself.

- Be patient with whom you are becoming. Don't try to recreate yourself overnight. Focus on one aspect at a time and make gradual improvements that will last a lifetime versus quick fixes that won't last two weeks.
- Develop your own "theories" based on the content of this book. Take what is useful, apply it to your life, and leave the rest behind.
- Don't rush out to share your new wisdom with all of your friends. Honestly, they may think you're crazy. If they do, it's not your fault. Everyone won't be ready to create a new mindset just because you are.
- As you read, make note of your "aha" moments. Feel free to write, underline, highlight, and mark in this book as needed. Make the most of it. Celebrate EVERY single accomplishment as you incorporate the lessons in your life. Every small change that you make or difference that you see in your life counts toward the big payoff. The more you celebrate, the more you'll have to celebrate.

Let's *WERK*!

xoxo

THE **WERK**ING

woman's

WAY OF LIFE

MINDSET MANTRA

STRAIGHTEN YOUR CROWN & embrace your throne

BE YOUR OWN BOSS

The statistics don't DETERMINE success...keep your eyes on the prize

PUT IN WERK

YOU ARE THE DESIGNER OF YOUR DESTINY

WATCH FOR THE SIGNS

PURSUE YOUR PASSION WITH PATIENCE, PERSISTENCE & POSITIVITY

USE YOUR FAITH TO TURN OBSTACLES INTO OPPORTUNITIES

SAY YES when it feels GOOD

TRUST YOUR INTUITION

LET LOVE lead YOUR LIFE

FOLLOW YOUR ♡ AND GOD WILL DO HIS PART

YOU ARE beautifully & abundantly blessed

THERE IS NO COMPETITION

You DON'T HAVE TO BEG BORROW OR SETTLE FOR ANYTHING

NOBODY CAN DO YOU LIKE YOU

WERK!

Prescriptions
NATURAL/HOMEOPATHIC
HEALTH & WELLNESS REMEDIES

Affirmations
POSITIVE PHRASES
THAT SHIFT YOUR MINDSET

Quotes
POWERFUL MESSAGES
THAT INSPIRE & EMPOWER YOU

Lifestyle Lessons
TIPS, TRICKS & TOOLS TO BUILD
YOUR PERSONAL BRAND, PURSUE
YOUR DREAMS & PUT YOURSELF FIRST

Journal Prompts & Worksheets
SUPPLEMENTAL EXERCISES
TO HELP YOU APPLY YOUR NEW KNOWLEDGE

A GAME - CHANGER DOESN'T LIVE BY THE RULES. SHE *CREATES* HER OWN

You only have one life to live, and it is time to start living, not just existing, but really living. Wake up everyday excited about the possibilities because you are creating the life you want. Break the rules that no longer serve you. When you release the opinions of others and stop limiting your abilities, you can focus on what you want and what makes

A GAME - CHANGER DOESN'T LIVE BY THE RULES. SHE *CREATES* HER OWN

you happy. You're now in position to cut the ties that bind you and finally write your own liberating rules. Learn to trust your instinct enough to know what works for you and what "rules" you want to live by.

When is the last time you let someone influence your actions? It could have been a subtle or subconscious influence. Write about a time that someone else's fears, desires, or wishes swayed a decision.

My Notes: _____

_____

_____

_____

_____

_____

_____

_____

2

CREATE A WEEKLY "TO-DO" LIST

Spend Sunday night creating a detailed plan for the week. I suggest adding the most important events to a time-management app, such as Google calendar (which syncs to your phone). Your "To-Do" list will be easily accessible and will keep you focused and on schedule.

ADD AFFIRM-ATIONS TO YOUR "TO-DO" LIST

There's power in the spoken word. I started this trick, and the results are AMAZ-ING. Add statements such as "Expect a contract," or "New partner-ship proposal or a happy surprise," and watch how quickly they will appear in your life.

4

GO ON A TIME-MANAGEMENT DIET

Where did the time go? If you've ever found yourself saying this, then you know how valuable time is. Once your time is gone, you can never get it back. Prioritize your life to ensure that you're spending every moment wisely. Get in the habit of tracking your time to see if it is being well spent or if adjustments need to be made.

"ALWAYS BE READY TO HAVE THE TIME OF YOUR LIFE. "

- UNKNOWN

5

MASTER THE "ONE-SONG" SHOWER

When I'm in a hurry, the one-song shower can be a lifesaver. I use it as my timer. When the song is over, my time is up.

My Notes: _____

_____

_____

_____

_____

TURN YOUR PAIN INTO A PAY-CHECK

Long story short. In 2010, I ended an engagement that became a toxic and abusive situation. After my then-fiance's efforts to diminish my self-esteem failed, I spent the next eight months on a journey of self-discovery. I channeled my physical and invisible wounds and delved myself into self-help books. What started as a single woman's mission to

TURN YOUR PAIN INTO A PAY-CHECK

search for answers and seek self-improvement, evolved into an international women's empowerment movement called The Single Wives Club™. Everything truly happens for a reason and the most successful entrepreneurs are those whose profit began as a problem. They're the ones who have a lesson to teach the world based on their personal experiences.

TURN YOUR PAIN INTO A PAY-CHECK

Identify your pain. Take an honest assessment of the lessons learned

There has been something in your life that probably caused a tremendous amount of pain and taught you a major lesson. Figure out the underlying message and find a way to teach it to the world. Have you been a victim of domestic abuse? Did you

6 CONTINUED

TURN YOUR PAIN INTO A PAY-CHECK

manage to lose a tremendous amount of weight for whatever reason? Have you mastered interviewing skills because of your stint with unemployment? If so, you've been given a special lesson to teach the world.

It was there all along
My lesson: I realized that I was unpre-

TURN YOUR PAIN INTO A PAY-CHECK

pared to become a wife because I had not fully become a woman. Through The Single Wives Club™, I'm now able to help thousands of single ladies become better women before becoming wives. Starting a membership-based organization with engaging workshops was easy. When I created a list of my gifts, talents, and skills, I realized that I've

TURN YOUR PAIN INTO A PAY-CHECK

always loved organizing people and planning events. For as long as I could remember, I've been organizing my friends, groups at school, events at work, etc. This is something I naturally do and love to do. I also discovered that part of my purpose is to educate and empower women. So, I've taken the training I received in obtaining my degrees along

TURN YOUR PAIN INTO A PAY-CHECK

with my experiences as an elementary school teacher to now create curriculums and plan lessons for the *WERK*shops I teach. Although I'm no longer a classroom teacher, the years dedicated to developing those skills were not lost, just redirected. Today, I'm receiving the payoff from the pain that I endured by organizing events for the purpose of

TURN YOUR PAIN INTO A PAY-CHECK

women empower-ment and self-develop-ment.

My Notes: _____

_____

_____

_____

_____

_____

_____

_____

Let's WERK! 💕

What skills and special training have you picked up along the way that you can use to launch a new career so you're in control?

What skills have you developed that you could use for profit?

What skills have you sharpened while working your 9-5? Get creative and find a way to profit from those skills. Whether you're a human resource specialist, computer technician, or even a nurse, you have skills and talents that can yield a profit.

What are you naturally good at doing?

What talents have you had since you were a child?

What are YOUR SKILLS?

My Notes: _____

_____

_____

_____

_____

_____

_____

_____

_____

_____

_____

_____

_____

_____

_____

_____

NATURAL/HOMEOPATHIC HEALTH & WELLNESS REMEDIES

" Ignorance is not bliss."

Whether you believe it or not, nature has a ton of vitamins and supplements that aid in optimal health. There are so many alternatives to prescriptions, copays, and "practicing" doctors. When my girl Jerri became a Master Herbalist, I asked her for a list of must-have vitamins and supplements. Below are five that she shared and that you should consider adding to your medicine cabinet. *Consider consulting your physician and/or do your research before taking any new supplements.*

Multivitamin. Multivitamins are essential to maintaining whole and complete health. However, whole food plant-based vitamins are preferred in this case. They are easy on the stomach and readily accepted by the body.

NATURAL/HOMEOPATHIC HEALTH & WELLNESS REMEDIES

One-A-Day vitamins may not provide the body with enough dosage or too much at one time.

Probiotics. Putting the good bacteria back into the colon is difficult when we are constantly exposed to toxins and chemically processed foods. A healthy gut leads to a healthy immune system. At least 10 billion organisms and 8 different strains of good bacteria are pivotal to choosing a probiotic.

Fish Oil. Omega 3,6, and 9 are key to maintaining youthful skin, moisturized hair, strong

 Looks like it's time for a shopping trip!

joints, vision, and cardiovascular heart health. This supplement is often frowned upon due to the after-effects of smelly burping and its unpleasant taste. But good news. Supplements come flavored, and are now enteric-coated to prevent the fishy burping smell.

Grapefruit Seed Extract. Believe it or not, I found that this supplement works wonders for eczema. It is also used for high cholesterol, cancer, weight loss, and even fungal infections.

My Notes: _____

_____

NATURAL/HOMEOPATHIC HEALTH & WELLNESS REMEDIES

Maca Root. Nicknamed "nature's viagra" increases stamina and enhances energy. Women typically use maca for hormone imbalance, menstrual problems, depression, stomach cancer, and so much more.

My Notes: _____

_____

_____

_____

_____

D.A.R.E. TO DREAM

Determine your destination.

What do you want? You are the designer of your destiny. To achieve your goals, you have to be clear and know where you're going.

Apply the lessons you've learned.

It is not about what you know; it is about

D.A.R.E. TO DREAM

what you do. To bring your dreams to life you must apply all of your new knowledge. In other words, put in the *WERK*.

Refuel your faith frequently.

Faith comes by hearing. This may mean weekly church services, daily meditation and journaling, or hourly affirmations.

D.A.R.E. TO
DREAM

**Educate
yourself.**

In order to live a
life you love, you
must become a
lifelong learner. The
more you know, the more
you'll grow.

My Notes: _____

_____

_____

Life rewards me everyday, happy *surprises* are on the way.

8

SIX POSITIVE WAYS TO START YOUR DAY

Inspired by Diamonde Williamson Author

1. Laugh.
2. Visualize a beautiful day ahead.
3. Affirm yourself.
4. Read a few pages from an inspiring book.
5. Write a few sentences in your gratitude journal.
6. Speak a few words of thanks ALOUD to your Creator.

9

A SALAD A DAY KEEPS THE DOCTOR AWAY

One thing we commonly leave out of our diet is raw food. By eating a salad each day, we assist our bodies in breaking down the other foods we consume.

My Notes: _____

_____

_____

_____

Let's WERK! ♡♡

7-DAY SALAD CHALLENGE

Eat a salad each day for 7 days and take note of any changes you experience.

Day 1:
_____

Day 2:
_____

Day 3:
_____

Day 4:
_____

Day 5:
_____

Day 6:
_____

Day 7:
_____

"STOP LETTING

SMALL-MINDED

PEOPLE TELL

YOU THAT YOUR

DREAMS ARE

TOO BIG."

- KOE

10

YOU DON'T HAVE TO CHASE WHAT GOD SENT

What is meant for you is already yours. You will not be required to beg, borrow, or steal. Here's a simple rule to always remember: If you have to force it, it isn't for you.

My Notes: _____

_____

_____

_____

11

BE A
CHAMELEON

Who will you be today? When I am hosting an event, I know that I must be friendly, outgoing, and helpful. When I am running a meeting, I know that I must be serious, firm, and knowledgeable. When I am out with my friends, I know I can be silly, wild, and fun. Be a chameleon, and let your environment dictate your character.

NATURAL/HOMEOPATHIC HEALTH & WELLNESS REMEDIES

Most Common Crystals

Crystals have been used for healing the body, transforming the spirit, inspiring intuitive insight, guarding against negative vibrations, and smoothing the energy flows of spirit and body.

According to Ancient Feng Shui, the power of the crystal can be found in its structure – growing and reaching up toward light from the deepest parts of earth. It is a conductor of energy– both as a receiver and a transmitter. Your personal crystals will attune themselves to your vibrations, as you will attune to the natural vibrations of the crystal.

" Crystals have been used for healing the body…"

NATURAL/HOMEOPATHIC HEALTH & WELLNESS REMEDIES

It is important to keep your crystal clean in order to protect it from outside negative vibrations. Certain colors are used in healing and magical manifestations with specific effects. For best results, choose crystals that speak to you or that you feel attracted to.

Red: Grace, purification, tolerance, patience, focus, acceptance, passion, healing guilt, blame, and anger.

Orange: Surrender, spiritual presence, valor, spontaneity, discrimination, happiness, joy, and enthusiasm.

Yellow: Gratitude, creativity, individuation, focus, inspiration, inventiveness, strength, courage, and individuality.

Green: Contentment, harmony, serenity, peace, balance, generosity, empathy, and temperance.

Blue: Charity, devotion, compassion, reciprocity, intelligence, humility, heart wisdom, and purity.

Indigo: Mercy, forgiveness, integration, wisdom, justice, intuition, synthesis, and structure.

" Your crystals will attune themselves to your vibrations..."

NATURAL/HOMEOPATHIC HEALTH & WELLNESS REMEDIES

Violet: Joy, freedom, abundance, detachment, centeredness, fairness, responsive, fortunate, and inclusive.

White: Integration, wholeness, foundation, spontaneity, cycles of fertility, potential, clarity, receptivity, and directness.

My Notes: _____

_____

_____

_____

_____

MIRACLES
& money
find me wherever I go.

12

DON'T FEED THE FEARS

There are two emotions from which many others originate: FAITH and FEAR. We can either have faith that things are always working in our favor, or we can surrender to fear. Today, I encourage you to let faith lead you toward the direction of your dreams. Expect the fears to surface, but be determined not to feed them with your attention. The next time

DON'T FEED THE FEARS

fear knocks, let faith answer the door.

My Notes: _____

_____

_____

_____

_____

_____

_____

_____

Let's WERK!

What is the one thing you've been putting off or haven't found the courage to do? Make a list of action steps and start working to get it accomplished. Ain't nothin' to it but to do it.

My Notes: _____

_____

_____

_____

_____

_____

_____

_____

13

"NO" MEANS NOT YET

You are
guaranteed
to experience
more than a few
"no's" along your
journey. One thing
that you can guarantee
is that no one has the po-
wer to deny you anything
you truly desire, unless you
give them permission to. When
someone tells you "no," it doesn't
mean it can't be done. It simply
means it can't be done with them.
Each day is a new opportunity to turn

"NO" MEANS NOT YET

those "no's" into "yeses."

My Notes: _____

_____

_____

_____

_____

_____

_____

_____

Let's WERK! 💕

Write about a time when things didn't go as planned, you faced an unforeseen obstacle, yet came out on top.

My Notes: _____

_____

_____

_____

_____

_____

_____

_____

_____

_____

14

ASSETS VS. LIABILITIES

Self-awareness is everything, and it is better to be responsible for how you act before someone else has the opportunity to bring it to your attention. In an effort to save face, complete this quick exercise to reveal something new about yourself. It is my signature "selfie check" that will help increase your self-awareness.

Let's WERK! ♥♥

ASSETS/LIABILITIES LIST

Your assets are the qualities, skills, and characteristics that add value to your life. Your liabilities are the areas that need improvement.

Check yourself.

1. Create a list of "I am good at" and "I need improvement in" statements.
2. Choose your 10 best traits and 10 need-most-improvement traits. Choose three areas to focus on improving, and create a plan for each.
3. Focus on all ten of your assets and find new ways to make them work for you.

Let's WERK!

My Notes: _____

_____

_____

_____

_____

_____

_____

_____

_____

_____

_____

_____

_____

_____

_____

_____

15

GET YA MIND RIGHT

You can't create new experiences with an old mindset. Make an effort to read a new book each month and meditate daily. For free meditation resources visit www.meditation-oasis.com

My Notes: _____

_____

_____

Let's WERK! ♡

Make a goal to meditate for at least 10 minutes each day for 7 days. Take notes of the positive changes you experience.

My Notes: _____

_____

_____

_____

_____

_____

_____

_____

_____

_____

_____

_____

"WITH EVERY

RISING OF

THE SUN,

THINK OF LIFE

AS JUST BEGUN. "

- UNKNOWN

16

YOUR HEALTH IS YOUR WEALTH

Without your health, all other goals are unattainable. Make a conscious effort to take better care of yourself by tracking what you eat and how it makes you feel. Think outside of the prescription bottle by researching an alternative to a medical doctor. Most major cities have integrative health centers that offer more than just prescriptions. They combine Eastern and

YOUR HEALTH IS YOUR WEALTH

Western medicine to provide a holistic approach to health and wellness. Some great wellness practices include: reflexology, iridology (eye reading), ionic foot detox, vaginal steaming, and acupuncture.

Natural Healing

I once met a woman who had spent $19,000 on fertility treatments. She later

YOUR HEALTH IS YOUR WEALTH

heard about acupuncture and got pregnant after three months of treatment. Then there's a woman who healed herself from fibroids with crystal healing therapy. I know these two women person- ally, so imagine how many other women around the world found success outside of the traditional doctor's office or hospital visits.

YOUR HAPPINESS IS IN YOUR HANDS

Not theirs, but yours. No one has the power to make you happy but you. When you put your happiness in someone else's hands, they will disappoint you every single time. It is literally impossible for someone to "make you happy." Your happiness depends on you alone.

Finding my purpose gave me that "in

YOUR HAPPINESS IS IN YOUR HANDS

love" butter-fly-in-my-belly feeling that I'd been chasing in men for so long. It was truly priceless. I want to encourage you to dig deep to find the courage to be happy.

Here are five ways to own your happiness:

1. Stop telling the same old story, it is time to write a new one.

YOUR HAPPINESS IS IN YOUR HANDS

2. Don't subject yourself to solitary confinement. Put value in developing relation-ships.
3. Balance it out. *WERK* hard; Play hard.
4. Enjoy the journey and appreciate the process.
5. Be patient with yourself.

18

PUT YOUR PRIDE ASIDE

Pride goes before a fall (Proverbs 16:18) Stop being too good to ask for help and too strong to be vulnerable. If you know you're going through something that is beating you up and on the verge of breaking you down, then get help. When you can't release negative thoughts out of your mind and find yourself replaying past failures over and over in

PUT YOUR PRIDE ASIDE

your
head, you
are literally
stopping
yourself from
enjoying life. You're
blocking your blessings
and sabotaging your
success. Stop putting
yourself in solitary confine-
ment and get the assistance
you need. You owe it to yourself to
invest in both your mental and
emotional health. There are a million
coaches, therapists, and support groups

18 CONTINUED

PUT YOUR PRIDE ASIDE

in your area. Need a therapist? Here are two I highly recommend:

Nikhol B. Jackson,
Transformational Coach
Nikholbjackson@gmail.com

Shaneka McClarty,
Licensed Therapist
Smcclarty@therapygirl.net

All the money
I spend now
comes back
to me
multiplied.

19

PUT IN
WERK

You can WISH or you can *WERK*. Nobody is handing out success. You gotta go out and get it. Dedicate yourself to your dream by spending one full hour each day building your brand and *WERK*ing toward accomplishing your goal. Did you know that one hour is only 4% of your day? You owe yourself at least that. Use this time to research, write,

PUT IN WERK

conduct
meetings,
send emails,
etc.

*Discipline yourself
for 30 days and
watch your business
grow.*

When I teach my *WERK*-
shops, I always tell my students
how important it is to invest in
themselves and their future. My
favorite phrase is "You can WISH or
you can *WERK*."

19

PUT IN
WERK

WERK is a term that I use to refer to the time and effort dedicated to your dream. It's the energy used to design your destiny. It's the time after working your corporate job that you spend building your personal brand. It's the commitment to reading books to enhance your craft. All these are what I call putting in *WERK*.

PUT IN
WERK

When
you're able
to find time
each day to
invest in yourself,
you will begin to see
major payoffs. You've
heard that anything worth
having is worth working for.
With all of the lessons you've
learned, you owe it to yourself
to live a life you love.

Track your time. Record how much time you spent *WERK*ing toward your dream each day for 30 days and watch how quickly you accomplish your goals.

SUN	MON	TUE	WED	THU	FRI	SAT

ACT AS THOUGH YOU ALREADY ARE

You are who you say you are. One of my favorite *WERK*ing women Patrice C. Washington, The Wisdom & Wealth Money Maven spoke life into her brand by introducing herself as a bestselling author even before her book was complete. She literally spoke her position into existence. You are who you say you are even if people can't see it yet.

20 CONTINUED

ACT AS THOUGH YOU ALREADY ARE

Practice what you want to experience, and it is guaranteed to show up in your life.

My Notes: _____

_____

_____

_____

_____

_____

_____

Let's WERK! 💕

There is POWER in belief. Use your imagination to visualize the woman you're becoming and then start acting like you're already her.

Give her a few attributes:
What is she doing?
Where is she going?
Who is she spending time with?
Then start acting the part and soon it will be so.

My Notes: _____

_____

_____

_____

_____

_____

21

LEAVE IT OR
BELIEVE IT

Many times we over-think, worry, and doubt ourselves right out of our blessings. The toughest part is learning to trust the process. Once you've mastered that, the world is yours.

My Notes: _____

_____

_____

22

WHY WORRY? IT PROBABLY WON'T HAPPEN ANYWAY

Instead of being pessimistic and worrying about what could go wrong, focus your energy on the possibility of what could go right. Worrying doesn't add another second to your life. Begin each experience with a positive expectation, and you will achieve a positive outcome. When you find yourself concerned or full of anxiety, learn to let go and let God.

NATURAL/HOMEOPATHIC HEALTH & WELLNESS REMEDIES

Apple Cider Vinegar

Apple Cider Vinegar (ACV) is literally a miracle juice. It smells gross and tastes bad, but ACV is a lifesaver. There's nothing more versatile, natural, and affordable. Not only does it have major health benefits, it also has several household uses. Some people like to take a shot of ACV, but I prefer to mix 2 tablespoons in a bottle of water and drink it throughout the course of the day. My favorite brand is Bragg's, which can be found at almost every health food store and even your local grocery store. During an episode of Dr. Oz, he talked about a bunch of new uses for ACV, and after a quick Google search, a zillion more uses were revealed.

My Notes: _____

_____

NATURAL/HOMEOPATHIC HEALTH & WELLNESS REMEDIES

Here are a few ways to use ACV:

For skin, teeth, and hair:
- Use as a hair rinse to fight dandruff and add body and shine
- Use as a facial cleanser to boost the pH balance of your skin
- Add to bath water to relieve the redness and pain of sunburn
- Reduces buildup on the scalp
- Helps in the removal of warts
- Reduces swelling and fades bruising
- Skin toner for blemishes
- Reduces cellulite
- Helps control bad breath
- Whitens teeth and kills mouth bacteria
- Use as an overnight soak to clean dentures

NATURAL/HOMEOPATHIC HEALTH & WELLNESS REMEDIES

For health:

- Use as a detox to cleanse the kidneys
- Drink or supplement to prevent flu
- Reduces inflammation from arthritis
- Relieves sinus pressure and fights infection
- Aids weight loss by decreasing appetite and increasing fat burn
- Relieves allergies and asthma symptoms
- Relieves gout
- Balances the body's pH level
- Lowers cholesterol
- Reduces blood glucose level in diabetics
- Removes nail fungus
- Soothes bug bites and other minor skin irritations
- Aids digestion
- Taken with warm water and honey before

NATURAL/HOMEOPATHIC HEALTH & WELLNESS REMEDIES

bedtime, ACV may help with sleep issues

- Strengthens bones
- Has anti-inflammatory properties
- Relieves pain from jellyfish stings
- Aids in relieving chest congestion
- Promotes bowel movements and eases constipation
- Relieves heartburn
- Can help stop hiccups
- Promotes sinus drainage
- Treats ear infections
- Soothes rashes
- Helps control sugar cravings
- Helps cure strep throat

"...There's nothing more versatile, natural or affordable!" - on Apple Cider Vinegar

NATURAL/HOMEOPATHIC HEALTH & WELLNESS REMEDIES

- Helps treat eczema
- Increases energy and boosts metabolism
- Relaxes sore muscles
- Disinfects wounds
- Boosts immunity
- Lowers blood pressure

For the home:
- Use as a natural disinfectant cleanser
- Use it to wash windows to leave a streak-free shine and clean scent
- ACV is a natural deodorizer
- Use it to deter cats from having accidents (they won't urinate where they smell vinegar).

My Notes: _____

_____

"GOD NEVER LETS YOU TAKE A LOSS. CONSIDER IT A LESSON LEARNED."

- KOE

WHY WORRY?
IT PROBABLY
WON'T
HAPPEN
ANYWAY

Everything is unfolding perfectly at the perfect time.

My Notes: _____

_____

_____

_____

_____

_____

_____

_____

When you find yourself feeling anxious or worried, shift your focus to a situation or person that makes you feel good about your life. It could be a recent promotion, a past weekend getaway, or a new relationship or friendship. Whatever comes to mind are your triggers or shifters that change your mood when you find yourself overly concerned.

Make a list of those triggers to refocus your thoughts on a better outcome or result. Things will start working out **more** when you start worrying *less*.

My Notes: _____

_____

_____

List Your
TRIGGERS

My Notes: _____

_____

_____

_____

_____

_____

_____

_____

_____

_____

_____

_____

_____

_____

_____

_____

_____

I create a
MASSIVE & PASSIVE
wealth.

23

REMAIN UNBOTHERED

You may not be able to control your circumstances, but you're certainly in control of your responses to them. When life hits, straighten your crown and don't step down from your throne for anyone.

My Notes: _____

_____

_____

ACT LIKE A LADY: 8 WAYS TO IMPROVE YOUR ETIQUETTE

1. Learn to listen with your mouth closed.
2. Always send thank you notes to show gratitude and appreciation.
3. Appropriately tip your waitress, valet, hairstylist, and any other service worker who is allowed to accept gratuity (10%-20%).
4. Turn your phone on silent and put it away during meetings and meals.

ACT LIKE A LADY: 8 WAYS TO IMPROVE YOUR ETIQUETTE

5. No business calls before 9 a.m. or after 9 p.m.

6. Save the gossip for your girlfriends. Don't get caught being catty in public.

7. Do NOT show up late for yoga or meditation class and try to sneak in quietly. It is an impossible task and it will annoy your teacher.

8. Facetime should be a personal, private conversation. The world doesn't

ACT LIKE A LADY: 8 WAYS TO IMPROVE YOUR ETIQUETTE

need to hear or see your video chat with your boo. Keep those conversations private (this rule applies to talking to bae on speaker phone, too).

My Notes: _____

_____

_____

25

TRUST THE TIMING OF YOUR LIFE

The same God who made a way last time will make a way this time.

My Notes: _____

_____

_____

_____

_____

_____

_____

26

WOW THEM WITH THE 30 SECOND RULE

*Inspired by
John C. Maxwell, Author
of "25 Ways to Win
with People*

Within the first 30 seconds of a conversation, say something that leaves a lasting impression. This is a simple way to make an easy connection. People everywhere need encouragement, and it doesn't take much effort to make someone's day. Plus, we never forget the people who make us feel good. Remember these words from Dr. Maya Angelou, *"I've*

26 CONTINUED

WOW THEM WITH THE 30 SECOND RULE

Inspired by:
John C. Maxwell, Author
of "25 Ways to Win
with People"

learned that people will forget what you said, people will forget what you did, but people will never forget how you made them feel."

My Notes: _____

_____

_____

27

SHARE YOUR
STORY

Each and every one of us has a unique set of experiences, an interesting perspective, and an exciting story to share. Even if you're not interested in becoming an author, there's no reason you shouldn't start a blog. Blogs are a great way to share your thoughts and connect with like-minded people who appreciate your perspective. *Plus, blogging can*

SHARE YOUR STORY

be an additional stream of income once you begin increasing your audience of influence.

My Notes: _____

_____

_____

You can literally blog about ANYthing you want and easily get started for free.

Not sure where to start? Here are five questions to help you find your voice as a blogger:

What are a few topics that have always interested you?

List 3-5 subjects that you are very knowledge-able about.

List the industries you have worked in.

What types of blogs do you read?

What type of people do you follow on social media?

Review this list and look for a pattern or

common trend. Use these results to select interesting topics you can begin writing about today.

My Notes: _____

_____

_____

_____

_____

_____

_____

_____

_____

_____

_____

_____

NATURAL/HOMEOPATHIC HEALTH & WELLNESS REMEDIES

Are You Good to Go Down Below?

In reference to American women who uses tampons, the average amount totals about 16,800 in a lifetime, according to The Huffington Post. Keep in mind that I know that this is a highly debatable topic. But, have you ever stopped to consider how tampons affect your health? During a vaginal steam session, an herbal-infused detoxing treatment that targets the vaginal area, the Certified Womb Sauna Practitioner warned me about the dangers of tampons and pads. I love my lady parts, so I had to do a little research and what I found was startling. Here it goes:

- Tampons and pads contain pesticides.
- Most tampons sold in stores are chlorine-bleached and made 100% from rayon.

NATURAL/HOMEOPATHIC HEALTH & WELLNESS REMEDIES

- Tampons and pads with odor neutralizers and other artificial fragrances are nothing short of a chemical soup laced with artificial colors, polyester, adhesives, polyethylene, polypropylene, and propylene glycol, contaminants linked to hormone disruption, cancer, birth defects, dryness, and infertility.
- Sanitary pads are subjected to the same considerations as tampons when it comes to the fibers and chemicals used to treat the fibers.

The bottom line? None of these chemicals should be anywhere near your body, let alone inside your body. But there is a cure. I would never list all of these jaw-dropping facts without giving you a solution. My favorite alternative to toxic tampons are (all-natural) herbal pads from Lhamo. These natural sanitary napkins are infused with five essential oils: Lavender (anti-inflammatory); Rose (pain relief); Mint (refreshing feeling); Aloe (moisturizing); and Houttuynia (antiviral). They create a safer alternative to the chemical-filled commercial pads we have used for years.

To order a pack of herbal pads visit:

www.ivpure.com

" I love my lady parts so I had to do a little research..."

28

TAME YOUR TONGUE

Inspired by:
Lakia Brandenburg,
The Wife Coach

The power of life and death lies within your words. Every word you speak creates your situation. Choose your thoughts, intentions, words, and actions carefully, and speak the life that you desire into existence.

My Notes: _____

_____

_____

29

SMILE. IT AWAKENS THE ANGELS

Awaken the angels in your life by greeting them with a genuine smile. A smile is the universal signal of happiness, and there's always someone watching you who has the power to bless you.

My Notes: _____

_____

_____

30

WHEN SOMETHING TELLS YOU, LISTEN

Have you ever said to yourself, "Something told me I shouldn't have …", or "Something told me I didn't need to …". When something tells you, LISTEN. Your intuition is a gift. It will never fail you if you learn to listen. The more you use your intuition and follow your instinct, the stronger it becomes. Go with your gut and learn to trust yourself.

CHECK YOUR SURROUNDINGS

Take a moment to analyze all the relationships you're in (friend-ships, family relationships, business partnerships, and romantic relationships) and figure out if you are gaining as much as you are giving or if you are taking more than you are giving. Everyone in your life is either an asset or a liability. It's up to you to remove and release anyone who no

CHECK YOUR
SURROUNDINGS

longer
adds value
or isn't moving
in the direction
of your dreams.

My Notes: _____

_____

_____

_____

_____

_____

_____

_____

Let's WERK!

Selfie Check

It's time for an attitude adjustment. What attitudes have you been carrying with you that you're ready to release?

In what ways can you improve your demeanor to make a better impression on others?

My Notes: _____

_____

_____

_____

_____

_____

_____

"FEAR KNOCKED AT THE DOOR BUT WHEN FAITH ANSWERED NO ONE WAS HOME."

- ENGLISH PROVERB

ATTITUDE IS EVERYTHING

Your
attitude
determines
your altitude,
and a kind spirit
can take you places
all the skills in the
world can't get you to. Be
conscious of how you come
across and communicate.
Make every effort to be friendly
and welcoming.

My Notes: _____

_____

_____

33

ACT LIKE ROYALTY AND THEY'LL TREAT YOU LIKE A QUEEN

People learn how to treat you based on how you treat yourself. When you hold yourself to a high standard, others will do the same. Act like the queen, expect nothing less, and watch people rise to the occasion.

My Notes: _____

_____

_____

MAKE APPOINT MENTS WITH YOURSELF

Inspired by
Deya "Direct" Smith, Author

Set aside time in your schedule to take care of yourself. Treat yourself to a solo date, attend a yoga class, or spend some quiet time reading your favorite book. Whether it's an hour or 24 hours, you deserve downtime.

My Notes: _____

_____

_____

FALL IN LOVE WITH YOUR LIFE

Inspired by:
Charreah Jackson,
ESSENCE Magazine

"A woman turned on by her life is irresistible to the world."

Be content with where you are right at this moment. Find something that brings you joy that doesn't require the company of someone else. When you're passionate about something, your life has more meaning.

List 10 things you love about your life:

1: _____

2: _____

3: _____

4: _____

5: _____

6: _____

7: _____

8: _____

9: _____

10: _____

I am *always* in
the right place
at the right
time.

36

BE AUTHENTIC

When you're truly comfortable in your own skin, you allow the world to love you as you are and appreciate your genuine spirit.

My Notes: _____

_____

_____

_____

_____

Let's WERK! ♡♡

What is there to love about you? What are you
really proud of?

My Notes: _____

_____

_____

_____

_____

_____

_____

_____

_____

_____

_____

_____

NATURAL/HOMEOPATHIC HEALTH & WELLNESS REMEDIES

Live BV Free

I remember having a conversation with different women who have been treated for Bacterial Vaginosis (BV), a smelly vaginal discharge that affects women. What is even more disturbing about this common infection is that doctors nor experts can ever tell you the exact cause or cure for the unwanted recurring discharge.

At one time in my young adult life, I suffered the shame of multiple infections. No matter what I did to treat the symptoms, nothing worked. Full of embarrassment, I paid the copay to go see a doctor to explain my symptoms, only to walk away with a prescription for one of those messy over-the-counter creams.

The medicine would clear up the infection for about a week and then the ole' faithful BV would return. This was one of the most annoying parts of the whole treatment process. I kept wasting money on "cures" that didn't work prescribed by a doctor who had no real answers.

The strangest part of this health scare was that it didn't matter whether I was sexually active or not. I would do anything to fight off the infection. I stopped using tampons and even switched soaps. After hours of Google research, I read countless stories from other

" I read [about] women who shared the same concerns with BV..."

NATURAL/HOMEOPATHIC
HEALTH & WELLNESS
REMEDIES

women who shared the same concerns with BV, and started taking bits and pieces from each success story to create my own.

Here's the magic formula that finally rid me of BV forever: *(Remember to consult a doctor before trying any new regimen.)*

Apple Cider Vinegar. *(I told you it's my miracle juice).* Take a shot of ACV in the morning or dilute it with water and sip on it throughout the day. It will help alkalize your body and balance your pH which means you are in a less acidic state. Trust me. Drink this every day and you'll start to notice the difference.

Take a Probiotic daily. Probiotics are the "good bacteria" that help promote normal vaginal pH. The most effective ones must remain refrigerated (e.g. yogurt).

Eliminate white sugar. Truth is, I have a serious sugar craving, but sugar is the culprit for thousands of ailments and illnesses (BV being one). The bacteria that combines to form BV actually feeds on sugar. In fact, it makes it grow rapidly. Make a healthier choice and replace white sugar with organic honey, agave, or another sugar substitute.

Garlic. Garlic is nature's antibiotic and can be taken at the first sign of infection. You can use it as a suppository or take it orally.

"IT'S NOT ABOUT

WHAT YOU KNOW,

BUT WHAT

YOU DO. "

- KOE

37

PURSUE
YOUR
PASSION

Most of the time your passion is connected to your purpose. You must actively pursue the things that excite you. Think about what makes you smile. What could you do everyday if you didn't get paid for it? What has always been your interest, but you never went after it?

Let's WERK! 💗

List 10 things that excite you:

1: _____

2: _____

3: _____

4: _____

5: _____

6: _____

7: _____

8: _____

9: _____

10: _____

38

GO ON A WORD DIET

Instead of watching your calorie intake, monitor your negative comments. Success-ful people speak great things into their lives because they expect only the best for themselves. They understand the power of their words and stay focused on positive thoughts rather than filling their minds and mouths with negativity. Spend the next seven days observing

GO ON A WORD DIET

your thoughts and pay close attention to your words. Be sure to only speak greatness into your life and immediately replace any negative thoughts with positive ones. Keep track of the difference it makes.

My Notes: _____

_____

_____

I am *beautifully* and **ABUNDANTLY** blessed.

SHOW YOUR SELF SOME LOVE (DAILY)

Here are 10 ways to promote self-love:

1. Do what feels good, not what looks good.
2. Treat yourself to a spa day.
3. Count your blessings and cast your burdens.
4. Stop asking for co-signers. Your approval is all that you need.
5. Let go of unhealthy habits.

SHOW YOUR SELF SOME LOVE (DAILY)

6. Stop speaking negatively about yourself.

7. Take compliments without a rebuttal.

8. Pursue your passion.

9. Set new goals.

10. Try something new.

TURN OFF THE TV

"Poor people have big TVs. Rich people have big libraries."
- Jim Rohn

One of the best ways to know that you are learning and growing each day is to read. Reading is the best way to become a lifelong learner. Learning new information and opening yourself up to new perspectives is a very effective way to guarantee yourself

40 CONTINUED

TURN OFF THE TV

personal and profes-sional success. After all, you're not a real BOSS unless all areas of your life are aligned mentally, physically, spiritually, financially, and professionally. Here are four entrepreneur favorites that are sure to inspire creativity, empower you to reach for the stars, and enhance your spirit.

TURN OFF
THE TV

**The Boss
Book List:**
Invest in your
intellect and
#ReadADamnBook.

**[MASTER THE MONEY
MINDSET]** *Think & Grow
Rich* by Napoleon Hill

If you have ever listened to
rapper Rick Ross' 2014 album,
Mastermind, it is filled with interludes
from this Napoleon Hill book. He is the
brilliant mind behind the "Mastermind

TURN OFF THE TV

Principle" (two or more minds working together in perfect harmony for a common objective). This Boss bible has been called the most important financial book ever written. Hill teaches about the relationship between money and the mind, sharing ways to enhance your ability to consciously create an intention to be successful and find financial freedom. The book outlines

TURN OFF THE TV

success
secrets
including
hundreds of
history's most
successful men,
from Andrew Carnegie
to Henry Ford. This is a
MUST-READ for anyone
who dares to dream big, and
grow rich at the same time.

My Notes: _____

_____

_____

40 CONTINUED

TURN OFF THE TV

[PERFECT YOUR PEOPLE SKILLS] *The Four Agreements* by Don Miguel Ruiz

This is a MUST-READ for personal development. It is nearly impossible to be successful in business when your thoughts are not aligned with your intentions. In *The Four Agreements*, Don Miguel Ruiz shares four principles to create love and happiness in

TURN OFF
THE TV

your life.
He also
shares an
in-depth look at
how we developed
our personalities,
prejudices, and beliefs
based on what we
experienced as children.
This book will help you reveal
your deficiencies and replace
them with positive alternatives
with four principles everyone can
appreciate.

TURN OFF
THE TV

[MAKE
YOUR
MONEY WERK
FOR YOU]
Rich Dad, Poor Dad
by Robert Kiyosaki

Referred to as the #1
personal finance book of all
time, *Rich Dad, Poor Dad* tells
the childhood story of money
principles learned from a rich father
and a poor father. Author Robert
Kiyosaki teaches money saving,
making, and investment principles that he

TURN OFF
THE TV

learned
from the
failures and
successes of his
father and his best
friend's father. This
book will change your
perception of money and
intensify your desire to
dream big and make your
money *WERK* for you.

[GET YA MIND RIGHT]
The Traveler's Gift by Andy Andrews

TURN OFF THE TV

The only fiction book to make The Boss Book list is *The Traveler's Gift* by Andy Andrews. Through colorful stories and exciting adventures, he shares valuable life lessons that will determine personal success and offer you a greater insight and appreciation of LIFE. From seeking wisdom to choosing happiness and being a person of action, you are guaranteed to take

TURN OFF THE TV

away a valuable lesson that will aid in your personal and professional success. Wealthy people enjoy learning new things every single day. More important, they consciously apply their newfound knowledge because knowing something without taking action means nothing. While it is important to take-in new information, be

TURN OFF THE TV

sure to apply it with new actions and intentions. No time to read? Purchase the audio-book or invest in a Kin-dle (which has an awe-some feature that will read the book aloud). Another great way to add excitement to educa-tion is with a group of friends. Start a local reading group or join an online book club and connect with women who can share in the learning experience.

Suggestions from
The Boss Bookshelf

- *4-Hour Workweek* by Timothy Ferriss
- *The Psychology of Winning* by Denis Waitley
- *The Game of Life & How to Play It* by Florence Scovel Shinn
- *Ms. Typed* by Dr. Michelle Callahan
- *The Alchemist* by Paulo Coelho
- *How to Win Friends and Influence People* by Dale Carnegie
- *Goal Digger* by Alicia Dunams

BAD CREDIT AIN'T BOSSY

Inspired by:
Amita Johnson,
Certified Credit
Consultant

Many times we suffer blows to our credit score due to pure ignorance. We simply do not know that the decisions we make with our money today are hurting our chance for a secure financial future. When it comes to marriages, financial issues are among the top reasons for divorce. I definitely want to avoid having an awkward and embarrassing

BAD CREDIT AIN'T BOSSY

*Inspired by:
Arnita Johnson,
Certified Credit
Consultant*

conver-
sation with
a potential
husband about
my low credit
score and high debt.
It's time to be proactive
by becoming financially
fluent before you jump the
broom.

*Did you know that only 1% of
Americans have an 800+ credit
score? Calm down if you are nowhere
close. Arnita Johnson, an advocate for*

BAD CREDIT AIN'T BOSSY

*Inspired by:
Arnita Johnson,
Certified Credit
Consultant*

*consumer
credit
awareness,
says that a good
score ranges
between 640-700.*

4 Steps to Credit Repair

1. Order Your Credit Report
You are entitled to one free
copy of your credit report from
three national credit bureaus each
year. It is important that you actually
know what is on your report to make

BAD CREDIT AIN'T BOSSY

Inspired by:
Arnita Johnson,
Certified Credit
Consultant

sure that your information is up-to-date and accurate. If you are like me and want to fix your credit, visit www.AnnualCredit-Report.com to order your credit report and get to *WERK*.

2. *Avoid being 30 Days Late*

It takes 12 months to redeem yourself from one payment that is 30 days late.

BAD
CREDIT
AIN'T
BOSSY

Inspired by:
Arnita Johnson,
Certified Credit
Consultant

Three 30-day late payments can negatively affect your overall credit score just as much as a bankruptcy. Pay at least your minimum payment by its due date. If at all possible, pay a little more than the minimum amount.

3. *Credit Cards Count*
Credit cards have the largest impact on your credit score. A secured credit

BAD CREDIT AIN'T BOSSY

Inspired by
Arnita Johnson
Certified Credit
Consultant

card
uses your
funds as
opposed to
lending funds with
interest. Please
note: These (revolving)
accounts do not ever
close on their own. You or
the lender must choose to
close it.

4. *Never Settle a Debt with a Collection Agency*
Unless they are able to prove that the

BAD
CREDIT
AIN'T
BOSSY

Inspired by:
Amita Johnson,
Certified Credit
Consultant

debt is accurate and actually yours, refuse to settle. Many times third parties purchase your debt without the proper documentation needed to collect because uneducated and uninformed consumers often pay without requesting proper proof. Don't be a victim!

42

DON'T TAKE IT PERSONAL JUST BLAME THE RETRO GRADE

Whether you're into "astrology" or not, I'm almost certain you've felt the effects of Mercury's Retrograde. Retrograde is when the planet appears to be moving in reverse which causes different aspects of our lives to "move in reverse." Freaky stuff happens during retrograde: Two of my friends got into car wrecks, I found myself arguing a whole lot with

DON'T TAKE IT PERSONAL JUST BLAME THE RETRO GRADE

my man, and a few of my business deals folded. This shift can cause technical difficulties, breakdown in communication, and it can make business dealing extremely difficult.

The only reason I managed to survive with my sanity is because I was ready. I had mentally prepared for the BS. You can't control your circum-

DON'T TAKE IT PERSONAL JUST BLAME THE RETRO GRADE

stances; you can only control your response to them. So, when mercury starts wreaking havoc, how will you handle it? Technical difficulties with your phone, computer, car, or relationships? **Don't take it personal, just blame the retrograde.** Good luck and may the force be with you.

Do a quick Google search to find out when the next retrograde will be.

When it comes, take note of what you experience during the retrograde, and write a few ways you can prepare for the next.

My Notes: _____

_____

_____

_____

_____

_____

"IF YOU'RE SCARED
TO PLAY THE GAME
YOU'RE NEVER
GONNA WIN."

- KOE

43

"HOW YOU GONNA WIN WHEN YOU AIN'T RIGHT WITHIN?"

Lauryn Hill, Doo Wop (That Thing)

When you're completely comfortable and confident with who you are, there is no enemy that can defeat you. The one trait all winners must have is a positive mindset.

You get right within by believing in yourself, having faith in your superpowers, and not letting anyone stagger your success.

44

DARE TO DREAM (DREAM DAY)

Believing is seeing. In other words, if you want to convince yourself that your dreams can still come true, you'll have an easier time manifesting your desires if you first visualize the possibilities (before they exist).

My Notes: _____

_____

_____

Write about your Dream Day.

Where are you?

What are you doing?

Who are you doing it with?

What are you wearing?

Include as many details to create a vivid image in your mind.

Now, think about the ONE thing you can do that can get you one step closer to making that Dream Day a reality.

My Notes: _____

_____

_____

_____

_____

Proceed with your
DREAM DAY

My Notes: _____

_____

_____

_____

_____

_____

_____

_____

_____

_____

_____

_____

_____

_____

_____

_____

_____

WHO'S IN YOUR CIRCLE?

Birds of a feather flock together. You represent the five people you are closest to. When you are constantly making changes for the better, your circle will begin to change. You will notice your mindset shifting and your thoughts becoming more conscious. Make an effort to surround yourself with people who will hold you accountable for being great.

WHO'S IN YOUR CIRCLE?

You are your friends. They are not simply a reflection of you. The people you share your world with show you how you feel about yourself and what you really want out of life. Take a moment to assess your circle of influence. If they aren't working with you, they're working against you, and their time is up. They do not deserve anymore of your energy.

Let's WERK! 💕

Do you associate with people who are interested in living the comfortable life, or working toward the life of their dreams?

Make a list of five people you spend the most time with. Who do you share the details of your desires with and give the most of your energy to? Then ask yourself:

- Do they support my dreams and want me to succeed?
- Do they offer constructive criticism or just criticize me?
- How do they spend most of their time?
- Do they speak positively or negatively about their own lives?
- Are they complainers or conquerors?

Who are your ASSOCIATES?

My Notes: _____

_____

_____

_____

_____

_____

_____

_____

_____

_____

_____

_____

_____

_____

_____

_____

_____

_____

46

GIVE UP WHAT IS WEIGHING YOU DOWN

Resilience. It is one of the most important life skills to develop. You have to be able to respond well to loss and disappoint- ment and bounce right back. When you decide to improve your life, the first thing you begin to experience is loss. Pablo Picasso said, "Every act of creation is first of all an act of destruc- tion." In other words, the wrong things

GIVE UP WHAT IS WEIGHING YOU DOWN

(bad relation-ships, self-sabotage) always fall apart before the right things (healthy bonds, great opportunities) come together. Make an effort to accept loss as part of the process and trust that an AMAZING new replacement is on its way.

Let's WERK!

What are you willing to give up to receive all that you desire and deserve?

My Notes: _____

_____

_____

_____

_____

_____

_____

_____

_____

_____

_____

NATURAL/HOMEOPATHIC HEALTH & WELLNESS REMEDIES

Green Smoothies

Green smoothies are life-changing because they contain green leafy vegetables. Due to their high-content of antioxidants, these veggies may be one of the best cancer-preventing foods. Based on USDA reports, studies have shown that eating 2 to 3 servings of green leafy vegetables per week may lower the risk of stomach, breast, and skin cancer. These same antioxidants have also been proven to decrease the risk of heart disease.

" A green smoothie a day keeps the doctor away. "

NATURAL/HOMEOPATHIC HEALTH & WELLNESS REMEDIES

Here are five reasons to make green smoothies a part of your daily diet:

- Simple way to boost immune system
- Natural energy booster
- Packed with disease-fighting antioxidants
- Natural weight loss (when you include protein)
- The best fast food. You can make one in less than 10 minutes

For more info on green smoothies, visit:
www.simplegreensmoothies.com

THINK OUTSIDE THE PRESCRIPTION BOTTLE

47

**GIRLS
COMPETE
QUEENS
COLLAB
ORATE**

When
you are
operating in
your purpose,
there is no
competition. Nobody
can *WERK* your divine
plan like you. It was
created just for you. Don't
get caught up in competing
with anyone for anything
because what is meant for you is
already yours.

48

BE A
BLESSING

The only way to guarantee continuous blessings is to be a blessing to others. Serve those in need whenever possible, in whatever way possible. When you are blessed, it is your duty to pay-it-forward.

My Notes: _____

_____

_____

Blessing list: Write out a few ways that you can be a blessing to your family, friends, and community.

Make a blessing jar.
Decorate a box or jar and add blessings to it each day. No matter how big or small, each miracle and/or act of favor counts. At the end of the year, take them out one by one, and count your blessings.

My Notes: _____
_____
_____
_____
_____

Miracles & blessings
are making their way
to me right now.

GET COMFORTABLE WITH BEING UNCOMFORTABLE

Think about your most recent personal dilemma. Instead of wondering why something is happening to you, recognize that it is happening *for* you. Although the roadblocks we face can be painful, they are really catalysts for creativity and change. The experiences that cause the biggest breakthroughs are typically the ones that cause the biggest break-

49 CONTINUED

GET COMFORTABLE WITH BEING UNCOMFORTABLE

downs. Embrace the uncomfortable change, look forward to your transformed future, and go confidently in the direction of your dreams.

My Notes: _____

_____

_____

What was your most personal "dilemma?"

Can you identify an underlying lesson?

Write a few ways you can learn from this lesson to avoid revisiting it in the future.

My Notes: _____

_____

_____

_____

_____

_____

_____

_____

50

THERE'S NOTHING WRONG WITH BEING NEEDY

A need is something that is essential or extremely important. You should never feel bad for needing something from someone you are in a relationship with (including friendships and family relationships). The key is to find a healthy way to express that need to others so that it doesn't become a toxic dependence.

51

DON'T GET MAD, GET MOTIVATED

Turn your obstacles into opportunities by allowing your creative spirit to takeover. Instead of feeling helpless and disgruntled when I see others crediting from my *WERK*, I channel that energy into creating something new— something to keep them guessing. I've learned to use all of the ammunition around me (both good and bad) to inspire and fuel my success.

52

SPEAK WHAT YOU SEEK UNTIL YOU SEE WHAT YOU'VE SAID

Complaining is a choice. Just as you choose what to wear, you choose what to say. Your life experiences can make you better or bitter; the choice is yours.

My Notes: _____

_____

_____

Let's WERK! ♡♡

Go 24 hours without complaining (not even once) and watch what a difference it makes in your life. The best thing you can do for yourself is show appreciation for appreciation for appreciation (laugh out loud) for the things that you have instead of complaining about what you don't.

My Notes: _____

_____

_____

_____

_____

_____

_____

_____

I am an *irresistible*
magnet to great and
wonderful experiences.

53

MASTERMIND YOUR WAY TO A MILLION

Create a weekly, monthly, or bi-annual mastermind meeting with your Dream Team where you share your profitable ideas and brainstorm intensely to create a solid strategy for success with a group of like-minded people.

54

GET YA 'ISH TOGETHER

What do you have to offer? There's nothing worse than a woman who expects a man to bring everything to the table while she shows up starving and looking thirsty.

4 Steps to Getting Ya 'Ish Together:

1. *Get REAL.* Take some time to do a deep self-reflection. What are you doing

GET YA 'ISH TOGETHER

with your life? I mean *really*. How are you spending your time? Our habits shape our lives because we are what we consistently do.

2. *Be specific by choosing ONE area to focus on.* Don't try to become a new person overnight.

3. *Create a plan and write it out.* There's just something about seeing it on paper that impresses it in your

GET YA 'ISH TOGETHER

sub-conscious. What steps are going to take to achieve your goal? Your steps must be carefully calculated and followed. Start slow, remain steady, and you'll finish strong.

4. *Get to WERK.*

Start moving in the direction of your goal and don't ever stop. You can't get anywhere by standing still. As long as you are making consistent

GET YA 'ISH TOGETHER

strides (in the right direction), you are bound to succeed. I've found that as long as you are working toward *something*, you'll consistently see improvements in all areas of your life. Once you begin achieving goals, you will set larger ones and begin holding yourself accountable to the little voice in your head. You will learn to trust yourself and your instincts

GET YA 'ISH TOGETHER

because you will begin to see yourself as being successful. Successful people focus their energy on a specific goal and practice patience, persistence, and positivity until they achieve it.

My Notes: _____

_____

_____

55

ARE YOU A DRAMA QUEEN, TRAUMA QUEEN OR BEAUTY QUEEN?

What kind of Queen are you? Choose wisely.

Inspired by: Shaneka McClarty, Licensed Therapist

- **Drama** *[drah-muh, dram-uh]* noun. always mad, hard to deal with
- **Trauma** *[trou-muh, traw-ma]* noun. hurt, guarded and emotionally damaged
- **Beauty** *[byoo-tee]* noun. constantly seeking improvement, growth, and happiness

Let's WERK!

Write about a time that you were a drama or trauma queen.

Was there a better solution?

How can you handle things better next time?

My Notes: _____

_____

_____

_____

_____

_____

_____

You Are What You Eat

According to a study done by 9th Mind Media, ninety-three percent of the food we eat isn't even real. It has zero nutritional value and actually harms us more than it helps us. When it comes to your health, ignorance is not bliss. The only way we can nourish our bodies is by eating foods that are full of the nutrients we need. Dead foods are the chemical preservatives or food cooked with high heat that makes us sluggish, lethargic causing *"itis."* On the contrary, food is supposed to energize us and make us feel alive. In addition to how it makes us feel, the food we consume has also been linked to many of the illnesses and diseases we commonly suffer from. In my research to find the relationship between food and disease, I stumbled upon Alfredo Bowman,

better known as Dr. Sebi, a pathologist, herbalist, biochemist, naturalist, and founder of the USHA Research Institute in Honduras. He's credited with over 28 years of using natural remedies to successfully cure diseases deemed "incurable" by modern medicine *(Dr. Sebi's definitely Google worthy)*.

In order to make the most of our mealtimes, it is important to pack each meal with electric foods. An electric food is one that is completely natural, of the Earth, and is alive. Here's a list of electric foods to grab during your next trip to the grocery store:

Fruit (no seedless or canned): Apples, bananas, berries, mangos, oranges, peaches, pears, plum, melons, grapes, and cantaloupe.

Nuts: Raw almonds and almond butter, raw sesame seeds, raw sesame, Tahini butter, walnuts, and hazelnut.

Grains: Amaranth, Kamut, quinoa, rye, spelt, teff, and wild rice (black).

Greens: Kale, turnip, dandelion mustard greens, lettuce (all except iceberg), nopales (Mexican cactus), poke salad, and spinach (use sparingly).

Teas: Alvaca, anise, chamomile cloves, fennel, ginger lemon grass, red raspberry, and sea moss tea.

56

PERCEPTION IS REALITY

Today, I challenge you to check yourself by finding out how others perceive you. Take an inventory of your character by trying this little experiment and see what type of responses you get. Send a text message to three people and ask, "What are three words you would use to describe me?"

Let's WERK!

Write down the responses you collect.

What improvements can you make based on the responses you received? One small change can create a completely new perspective.

My Notes: _____

_____

_____

_____

_____

_____

_____

_____

WHO GON' CHECK YOU, BOO?

Take back your control. You are in control of your happiness and have every right to defend yourself (although it is not even worth it half the time). What we have to realize is that we are giving people the authority over us when we accept their criticism, negative opinions, or bad energy.

Figure out *your* feelings so others can't

WHO GON' CHECK YOU, BOO?

put theirs off on you. People will quickly realize who they can and can't push their negative energy off on. When they see that they can't affect you, they'll stop trying.

Don't be so quick to ask what they think. All the answers you need come from within. Learn to trust yourself more than you trust the opinions of

57 CONTINUED

WHO GON' CHECK YOU, BOO?

others. Learn self-control. A lack of self-control will lead to your suffering. Remember, you are not in control of circumstances, but you can control your reaction to them.

My Notes: _____

_____

Let's WERK! ♡

When was the last time you let someone influence your decisions?

What will you do differently next time?

My Notes: _____

_____

_____

_____

_____

_____

_____

_____

58

AVOID
NEGATIVE
NANCY

Misery loves company, and negative people love negativity. They won't be happy until you're unhappy, too. You know they're coming, so don't be surprised. Be ready and move out the way.

My Notes: _____

_____

_____

Let's WERK! 💕

Get REAL. Who brings negative energy anytime they are around?

Who annoys you, but you've become comfortable with the relationship?

My Notes: _____

_____

_____

_____

_____

_____

_____

_____

_____

59

YOU GET WHAT YOU GIVE

Karma is real! When you give good, you get good. Go out of your way to be good to someone today, and watch how quickly the favor is returned.

My Notes: _____

_____

_____

60

KNOW YOUR LIMITS

There are None.

My endless good now comes to me in endless ways. Today will be an amazing day.

COMPLIMENTS ARE CRUCIAL

Be flattering. Flirt with people everywhere you go by giving them genuine compliments. It is possible to find something you like about everyone. It's such an easy way to instantly brighten their day.

My Notes: _____

_____

_____

DARE
TO BE
BARE

Be transparent. Every once in awhile, go without makeup. You would be surprised by how many men actually prefer a natural look. When you're dating someone new, try showing up with no makeup *(I wouldn't recommend this on the first date because first impressions last forever).* But after you break-the-ice, be bold by showing him you're

DARE
TO BE
BARE

comfort-
able in his
presence and
confident in
yourself.

My Notes: _____

_____

_____

_____

_____

_____

WEALTHY PEOPLE DON'T WORK FOR PEOPLE

"If you don't follow your dreams, you'll end up working for someone who followed theirs." I understand that everyone does not aspire to become an entrepreneur. But I also realize that our generation has been trained to believe in the work system instead of being properly educated about the wealth system. Real wealth takes *WERK*.

WEALTHY PEOPLE DON'T WORK FOR PEOPLE

It takes time, dedication, effort, and energy to build a business into a successful company. But the same formula is very similar, if not equal to the work you are already putting into building someone else's business.

Still on the fence about whether you deserve to design your destiny and live a life that you love?

63 CONTINUED

WEALTHY PEOPLE DON'T WORK FOR PEOPLE

Here are five reasons to Be your own boss (BYOB)

1. The essence of life is in pursuing your purpose.

You may be a natural at your job, and you may even enjoy your work, but that doesn't mean you are pursuing your passion. You're only given a chance at living this life one time. Knowing this, why

WEALTHY PEOPLE DON'T WORK FOR PEOPLE

waste it wandering around aimlessly because you're stuck in the "cycle" or rat race of life: Work, home, sleep. Work, home, sleep.

2. **You owe it to yourself to follow your dreams and live life to the fullest with no regrets.** You deserve to see the fruits of your labor. There is nothing more disappoint-

WEALTHY PEOPLE DON'T WORK FOR PEOPLE

ing about working a corporate job for years and not seeing the fruits of your labor. After you've worked your fingers to the bone, spent your lunch hour at your desk, and missed your daughter's recital or son's tennis match all because of deadlines at work, do you receive anything more than a paycheck? Do you ever really see the benefits of

WEALTHY PEOPLE DON'T WORK FOR PEOPLE

busting your butt? I think not. As an entrepreneur, you directly benefit from all of your work. When you spend extra time on a project, you are rewarded with a loyal client. When you complete extra work, you get extra pay. Being your own boss puts you in control.

3. You can control your calendar.
Imagine being able to schedule your own

WEALTHY PEOPLE DON'T WORK FOR PEOPLE

meetings, choose which tasks are of most importance, and free up your time for the things you really want to do. That is the life you are afforded when you take a leap of faith into entrepreneurship. You may have to spend several late nights putting in *WERK*, but I guarantee it will be a completely different experience when you are on your own time.

WEALTHY PEOPLE DON'T WORK FOR PEOPLE

4. Live outside the box.

As an employee, you're forced to fit into the "corporate culture" and your personal freedoms are limited. You must dress within company standards, hide your personal imperfections for fear of termination, and behave the way they see fit so that you're properly representing their brand. Why not dictate your own life?

WEALTHY PEOPLE DON'T WORK FOR PEOPLE

You owe it to yourself to find your way out of the corporate box and elevate yourself to freedom. If you decide that you're finally brave enough to get that tattoo you've been wanting, you can make the appointment without fearing repercussions at work. Ready to try a new hairstyle? Have you thought about adding a pop of color or a spiky look to show off your

WEALTHY PEOPLE DON'T WORK FOR PEOPLE

personality? Then you should be able to do just that. As an entrepreneur, you are able to step outside of the norm and live by your own creative rules.

5. No salary cap.

How much money do you want to make? The one thing I despised about teaching was the fact that no matter how hard I worked, how much

WEALTHY PEOPLE DON'T WORK FOR PEOPLE

overtime I spent with my kids, or how well they performed academically, my paycheck stayed the same. I could've been crowned Teacher of the Year and received praises for my students scoring the highest on the state-mandated test, or the worst performing educator in my building with failing students. It didn't matter. My low salary was set. Not long

63 CONTINUED

WEALTHY PEOPLE DON'T WORK FOR PEOPLE

after this did I realize that the work system wasn't for me. And it is only a matter of time before hardworking and dedicated employees across the country understand how much more successful and profitable they could be if they got creative with their talents.

(See Lifestyle Lesson 6, Turn Your Pain into a Paycheck)

I now release
everything that is not
divinely designed
for me and create
space for all that
I deserve.

64

ENTHUSIASM IS EVERY THING

When you're excited about life, life greets you with excitement. Be optimistic about everything. Greet people and situations you face with joy, and you'll be amazed by how you are greeted in return.

My Notes: _____

_____

_____

65

INVEST IN
YOURSELF

Be very strategic with how you treat yourself. What are you putting in and on your body? What are you listening to? A dollar-menu diet yields a dollar-menu mindset.

My Notes: _____

_____

_____

66

EVALUATE YOUR VALUES

Most of our ideas, beliefs, and values have been passed down from our parents. We unconsciously follow their lead (sometimes for our entire lives) without questioning WHY we believe what we believe.

My Notes: _____

_____

_____

Update your definitions

How do you define love? Wealth? Success?
What does happiness look like to you?

My Notes: _____

_____

_____

_____

_____

_____

_____

_____

67

DEDICATE
A DAY

Choose a
day to set
aside and
spend with your
friends and family.
These are the
people who love and
support you. Remain
connected to them without
ruining your tight schedule.

My Notes: _____

_____

_____

Which day are you going to dedicate to your loved ones?

Who do you need to check-in with?

My Notes: _____

_____

_____

_____

_____

_____

_____

_____

_____

TAKE THE KOEK BOTTLE CHALLENGE

I took a personal health challenge and lost more than 20 pounds and dropped three dress sizes all from eliminating meat from my diet. But I still didn't have the shape I wanted. Since I'm super small up top with pretty wide hips, my ideal shape was the 'Coke Bottle' figure. My body literally remained the exact same shape, just smaller.

TAKE THE KOEK BOTTLE CHALLENGE

I couldn't believe I had lost so much weight, but still had a bad case of the muffin-top syndrome. In addition to losing my love handles, I also wanted to lift my butt. Going from weighing 155 to 135 pounds meant losing my butt. It was as if it completely fell off. Although I liked being called "skinny," I really missed being called, "thick." It was then that I

TAKE THE
KOEK BOTTLE
CHALLENGE

realized I had to be strategic and specifically target the areas I wanted to improve. So, I came up with a plan to get my ideal figure.

Step One: Eat veggies daily

When I was introduced to electric foods (energy providing foods that are all-natural and 100% living), I completely changed my diet. I'm not a

TAKE THE
KOEK BOTTLE
CHALLENGE

vegan or even a vegetarian because I still eat seafood. But, I eat mostly vegetables. My favorites are spinach, green beans, cabbage, and mushrooms. There's so many ways you can prepare a healthy veggie meal. I like to make a loaded veggie potato, add them as a side with rice or whole wheat pasta, or with shrimp or fish. I find creative ways to

TAKE THE
KOEK BOTTLE
CHALLENGE

make
them
delicious, and
it's so worth it.

**Step Two: Squats
no shots**
One thing I KNOW is that
if you do no SQUATS you
will have no butt. No matter
how much they hurt or how bad
you hate doing them, they really
work. Here's a bonus: Squats also
tone your overall body, not just your
butt.

TAKE THE KOEK BOTTLE CHALLENGE

Step Three: Apple Cider Vinegar (ACV) Did I mention that there are tremendous health benefits with this miracle juice? Of course, I did. And weight loss is no exception to this magical potion. By stabilizing blood sugar for a longer period, ACV helps cut cravings and controls the appetite. However, if your diet sucks, don't think a few teaspoons is

TAKE THE
KOEK BOTTLE
CHALLENGE

gonna do
the trick.
You may need
to revisit Step
#1.

Step Four: *WERK*out

Find a fun way to
workout the specific areas
of need. Search www.Grou-
pon.com to try out different
dance studios or fitness trainers.
You can even find a variety of
amazing at-home workouts on
www.YouTube.com.

68 CONTINUED

TAKE THE
KOEK BOTTLE
CHALLENGE

Step Five: Waist train

Say what you may, but I experienced great results using my waist trainer daily. Since my goal was to cinch my mid-area, this hourglass shaper was a good investment.

Disclaimer: Be sure to do your research before trying any new weight loss tricks.

···· I AM OPEN ····
TO RECEIVE
ALL THAT GOD
HAS FOR ME.
· · · · · · · · · · · · · · · · · · · ·

"NOTHING IS TOO GOOD TO BE TRUE; NOTHING IS TOO GOOD TO LAST WHEN YOU LOOK TO GOD FOR YOUR GOOD."

- KOE

CREATE A
WERK
SPACE

Make
your office
a sacred
space to create
magic. Here are
five MUST-HAVEs:

1. An inspiration wall

An inspiration wall serves
as a constant reminder of
what you're working toward. No
matter where you glance, your
eyes land on words that make you
feel good. Words like "Fearless,"
"Faith," "Imagine," and all things bright,

CREATE A
WERK
SPACE

colorful,
and bold
(just like me)
are what you'll
find in my *WERK*-
space. You can
include goals that
you've set for yourself,
positive affirmations,
prosperity post-it notes,
success catch-phrases, a vision
board and any other source of
inspiration that can keep you cool,
calm, collected, and connected when
the pressures of your workday arises.

CREATE A WERK SPACE

2. An idea note-book

My mentor once said, *"God is not required to repeat Himself. When He gives you inspiration, it is up to you to make the most of it."* I've spent years telling myself, I'll write it down later and let several great ideas slip away from me. These days, I will jot down an idea on any random piece of paper I can find, just to get it out of my

69 CONTINUED

CREATE A WERK SPACE

head. In my office, I keep a sacred million-dollar idea notebook. This one is specifically for the grand ideas I come up with that I will one day execute with ease. Invest in a notebook or journal that has an inspirational quote, a catchy phrase, or a neat design. Keep it with you wherever you go, so whenever you get a thought you can write it down.

CREATE A
WERK
SPACE

3. Reading material

Discover new things in a book. When you find yourself experiencing writer's block or letting your workload weigh you down, books are a great source of motivation. Some of my favorite titles that I can always count on when I'm in need of motivation and a quick reality check are *The Psychology of Winning* by Dennis Waitley and *The Game of Life*

CREATE A
WERK
SPACE

by Florence Scovel Shinn. Find a few that are meaningful to you and keep them on your office bookshelf.

4. Apple MacBook

Once upon a time, I was a diehard PC lover (before I become an entrepreneur). Over the years, my Macbook has been one of the best investments I've made. Applications like

CREATE A
WERK
SPACE

iPhoto, Garage-Band, and iMovie are ideal for any small business owner who deals with technology … and that would be ALL of us.

5. Wireless printer

Most often, entrepreneurs operate from their laptops and smartphones. If this is the case, having a wireless printer is less hassle and less time-

CREATE A
WERK
SPACE

consuming than a traditional wired printer. The other feature with wireless printers is you can connect multiple devices to it fairly easily and as you know, our goal is to *WERK* smarter and not harder.

My Notes: _____

_____

_____

70

YOUR REQUEST DETERMINES YOUR ROUTE

Starting route. We have all made the mistake of leaving off the NW or SW portion of an address and ending up at a completely different destination. The universe works just like a navigation system. The more accurate you are with the destination you input, the closer it will take you to it. If you can get clear about your goals, you will be able to get there much quicker

70 CONTINUED

YOUR REQUEST DETERMINES YOUR ROUTE

and on a much easier route. When you're unclear about where you're going, it is going to be very hard for God to send you the roadmap.

My Notes: _____

_____

_____

YOU ARE
WHAT YOU
ATTRACT

Like
attracts like
and energy is
everything. Dig
deep to figure out
what signals you've
been sending out. Your
mood, emotions,
thoughts, intentions,
actions, and words create the
energy that you send out into
the world and it is returned to the
sender every single time. If you
send out doubt, worry, and fear you
are asking for more reasons to feel

YOU ARE
WHAT YOU
ATTRACT

doubt, worry, and fear. Likewise, if you release love, happiness, and faith, get ready to receive an abundance of all the joy your heart can hold.

My Notes: _____

_____

_____

Let's **WERK!** 💕

What signals are you sending out to the universe? Take note of how people respond to you while you're out today.

How do strangers approach you? Do you notice that people are friendly and smiling at you, or are they moving out of the way when you walk by?

What type of men do you typically attract?

Do you attract loyal, trustworthy, honest men, or do you attract emotionally unavailable, unstable men? Remember, you are what you attract.

How can you improve your attitude to begin attracting more positive experiences?

Let's WERK! ♥♥

My Notes: _____

_____

_____

_____

_____

_____

_____

_____

_____

_____

_____

_____

_____

_____

_____

_____

_____

Let's **WERK!**

> ""*Everybody dies but not everybody lives.*""
>
> - *Drake, Moment 4 Life*

When was the last time you tried something for the first time? Create a Bucket List:

Are you living or merely existing? Make sure you're making the most of every single day you're blessed with by creating a bucket list. A bucket list is defined as a list of things you must do before you "kick the bucket" or die. So, have at it. Write down at least 10 things you MUST DO before you pass away and then get to it. Refer back to the list and check them off one by one.

What's Your
BUCKET LIST?

1: _____

2: _____

3: _____

4: _____

5: _____

6: _____

7: _____

8: _____

9: _____

10: _____

11: _____

12: _____

13: _____

14: _____

15: _____

YOU HAVE TO GET IN THE GAME TO WIN

Life is NOT a spectator sport. Stop sitting on the sidelines cheering on everyone else. Be the star player in your life and make big plays.

10 things winners do:

1.Winners take time for themselves every single day.

YOU HAVE TO GET IN THE GAME TO WIN

2. Winners turn off the TV and invest in their intellect.

3. Winners look their best at all times, so they can feel good at all times.

4. Winners are great receivers.

5. Winners take blame and credit honestly and openly.

YOU HAVE TO GET IN THE GAME TO WIN

6. Winners invest in themselves.

7. Winners focus on the positive until they can improve the negative.

8. Winners create healthy habits.

9. Winners associate with other winners.

YOU HAVE TO GET IN THE GAME TO WIN

10. Winners remain cool, calm, collected, and connected under pressure.

My Notes: _____

_____

_____

STRESS LESS.
SMILE MORE

According-
ing to the
American
Institute of
Stress, about
ninety percent of all
diseases, ailments,
and illnesses are consid-
ered stress related. So,
whether or not you realize
you're being affected by stress,
more than likely you are. There
are numerous stressors that may be
working your nerves, but the most
common ones are finances, bad relation-

73 CONTINUED

STRESS LESS.
SMILE MORE

ships, and a bad job. In fact, I read somewhere that a bad job can be more stressful than unemployment. You owe it to yourself to do whatever it takes to stress less and smile more.

My Notes: _____

_____

_____

Let's WERK!

Identify your stressors by answering these questions:

What do you spend the most time worrying about?

What people do you avoid spending time with?

What can you do to relieve your stress?

How can you avoid stressful situations?

My Notes: _____

_____

_____

_____

Identify your
STRESSORS

My Notes: _____

_____

_____

_____

_____

_____

_____

_____

_____

_____

_____

_____

_____

_____

_____

_____

_____

74

WERK.
PRAY.
SLAY.

Werk
Dedicate
your life to your
dreams

Pray
Ground yourself in faith

Slay
Show out in celebration of your
success

For the next 21 days, I will dedicate my life to

my dreams by _____.

I will ground myself in faith by

_____.

When I achieve my goal, I will show out in

celebration of my success by

_____.

♡ Goal Card

Successful people focus their energy on a specific goal and practice patience, persistence, and positivity until they achieve it.

Things you need:

A goal:

A deadline:

Action steps:

1.

2.

3.

4.

5.

Key people: _____

_____

Ways you will celebrate reaching your goals:

_____

_____

75

NOTHING HAPPENS BY CHANCE

You are always in the right place at the right time (if you get your mind right). When you're in your lane following your heart and pursuing your God-given purpose, the doors will swing open, the opportunities will find you, and the fear will fade away. **YOU have something in you** that's begging to get out and once you figure out what it is, you're going to be unstoppable.

CONSIDER YOUR CORE

Who you are at your core has ALWAYS been the same. There were so many clues from my childhood that I would be an entrepreneur. I was literally obsessed with working. I spent the weekends and summers "assisting" my dad at his office and when I turned 14, I lied about my age and got hired at the local McDonald's. I've literally been

CONSIDER YOUR CORE

*WERK*ing ever since. From daycare centers to banks and pharmacies, I've worked in every single industry, exploring my interests. It is no surprise that I'm still exploring them as a serial entrepreneur.

My Notes: _____

_____

_____

Let's WERK!

Spend some time rediscovering yourself.

- What clues can you gather from your childhood to discover your passion?
- What has always been an interest of yours?
- What have you loved doing for as long as you can remember?

My Notes: _____

_____

_____

_____

_____

_____

_____

YOU GET IT FROM YA MAMA

Whether you like it or not, you are probably a whole lot like your mother. If you're like most women, you've inherited her good and bad qualities. It wasn't until I read *Ms. Typed* by Dr. Michelle Callahan that I realized just how much I had picked up from my mom. Not only did I have her freckles, nose, and hips, but apparently I had her dating personality,

YOU GET IT
FROM YA
MAMA

too. While
reading this
book, I
realized that
what I saw in my
home as a little girl
had a great effect on
my adult life. The way my
mother handled stress
rubbed off on me. The way
she handled my dad rubbed off
on me even her outlook on life
seemed to affect mine.

This new info caused a major "aha"

YOU GET IT FROM YA MAMA

moment for me so I decided to dig a little deeper and analyze the good and bad traits I picked up from both of my parents. I realized why I never let a man "take care of me." I learned how I got to be so secretive and I even learned where my inappropriate laugh came from *(Thanks dad!)*. This newfound info shocked the hell out of me and what you're about to

YOU GET IT FROM YA MAMA

to learn
may sur-
prise you, too!

My Notes: _____

_____

_____

_____

_____

Let's WERK! ♡♡

Write at least three good qualities you picked up from your parents.

Write at least three bad qualities you've picked up from your parents.

How have these qualities shaped your experiences?

What steps can you take to start changing your beliefs?

My Notes: _____

_____

_____

_____

What are your
QUALITIES?

My Notes: _____

_____

_____

_____

_____

_____

_____

_____

_____

_____

_____

_____

_____

_____

_____

_____

_____

_____

it's time
TO PICK UP THE PIECES
DISCOVER
— YOUR —
Purpose
AND
GET-YOUR-LIFE-TOGETHER

 # WERK

CPSIA information can be obtained at www.ICGtesting.com
Printed in the USA
JW11s2118260116

458BV00049B/163/P